Edinburgh Trams, The Last Years Volume

by R.J.S. Wiseman BA

No. 290 (1923-1... ...Terrace at Coates... ...its way to the city centre and King's Road, Portobello. *3 July 1954.*

FOLLOW THE TRAM ROUTES ON LOTHIAN BUSES			
Tram service number and route	Tram abandonment date	Bus service number and destination	Notes
1, Corstorphine (Maybury)	27 March 1954	31, East Craigs	
2, 22, Stenhouse	13 December 1952	25, Riccarton	Originally bus service 22
3, Stenhouse	28 March 1953	3, 3A, Clovenstone	
4, Slateford	2 May 1953	4, Hillend	
9, 10, Colinton	22 October 1955	10, Torphin	Originally bus service 9 also
12, Corstorphine (Maybury)	10 July 1954	12, Gyle Centre	
24, Comely Bank	31 May 1952	24, Edinburgh Park; 29, 42 Silverknowes	Originally bus service 29
25, 26 Drum Brae South	10 July 1954	26, Clerwood	Originally bus service 25 also
27, Firrhill	6 August 1955	27, Hunter's Tryst	

Acknowledgements

I would like to thank all those who have assisted with the preparation of this book, especially John Meredith who printed many of the photographs, and George Fairley and Alastair Gunn for their help in checking text and captions. I would also like to thank those who have provided additional photographs as credited.

Further Reading

Brotchie, A.W., Edinburgh, *The Tramway Years*, N.B. Traction, 1979.
Brotchie, A.W., *The Twilight Years of the Edinburgh Tram*, Adam Gordon, 2001.
Hunter, D.L.G., *Edinburgh's Transport*, Advertiser Press, 1964.
Hunter, D.L.G., *Edinburgh's Transport, The Corporation Years*, Adam Gordon, 1999.
Stevenson, J.L., *The Last Trams*, Moorfoot Publishing, 1986.
Twidale, G.H.E., *A Nostalgic Look at Edinburgh's Trams Since 1950*, Silver Link, 1989.
Railway Magazine.

EDINBURGH'S TRAMWAYS – A BRIEF OVERVIEW

The first tramway in the City of Edinburgh was opened by the Edinburgh Street Tramways Co. on 6 November 1871 and ran from Haymarket via Princes Street and Leith Walk to Bernard Street in Leith. The company later extended its lines in Edinburgh and also in Leith and Portobello. On 9 December 1893 those lines in Edinburgh passed to the Corporation and were leased to Dick, Kerr & Co. Ltd, which formed the Edinburgh & District Tramways Co. in 1894 to run the system. Three years later, in 1897, the company took over the cable lines to Goldenacre and Comely Bank which had been opened by the Edinburgh Northern Tramways Co. in 1888 and 1890 respectively.

The older routes had been horse-hauled, and with the exception of the line to Craiglockhart, were converted to cable traction in 1899-1901. The last horse tram ran on 24 August 1907 when Craiglockhart was converted to cable operation. The Edinburgh & District Tramways Co. also opened an electric tramway, to Slateford, on 8 June 1910. Leith Corporation took over the horse tramways in their area on 23 October 1904 and converted these to electric traction between 18 August and 21 November 1905.

On 1 July 1919 the City & Royal Burgh of Edinburgh Transport Department took over the cable tramways and the electric line to Slateford. The Burgh of Leith was amalgamated with Edinburgh on 20 November 1920, at which point the Leith electric tramways came under the control of Edinburgh. Work then started on phasing out the cable system, and electric traction was introduced between Pilrig and Liberton on 20 June 1922. The last cable tram ran on 23 June 1923. In the meantime the ex-Edinburgh Northern cable tramways to Goldenacre and Comely Bank were variously replaced by buses.

Electric traction was introduced from Hanover Street to Goldenacre on 8 June 1924 and to Comely Bank on 18 November 1923. The city also purchased the Joppa to Levenhall section of the Musselburgh & District Electric Light & Traction Co.'s line on 7 May 1931, which it had operated since 1 March. Many extensions were built, although the line to Crewe Toll was never completed and authorised extensions from Fairmilehead to Hillend Park, Liberton to Kaimes, and Stenhouse to Sighthill were never built.

THE WESTERN TRAMWAYS

This is the third volume covering the tramways of Edinburgh as they existed between 1952 and their closure on 16 November 1956 and covers those routes which served the west and south-west suburbs and the route to Comely Bank, north west of the city centre. These can be divided into four main groups. First is the route to Comely Bank - service 24. Second are the routes from Waverley to Corstorphine – services 1, 12, 25 and 26. Third are the routes to Stenhouse and Slateford – services 2, 3, 4 and 22. Fourth are the routes to Firrhill and Colinton via the Mound – service 27 – or via Princes Street – services 9 and 10.

By 1952 the tram fleet in Edinburgh could be divided into two main classes – the old standard cars built between 1923 and 1934, and the new standard cars dating from between 1933 and 1950. All were four-wheeled enclosed cars, the older ones having wooden bodies and the newer ones being either all-steel or of composite construction. The latter were built in the Shrubhill Works except for 115 trams built by contractors as detailed in Volumes 1 and 2 of this series.

Trams ran to Comely Bank for the last time on 31 May 1952. No. 235 (1936-1956) is seen here at the terminus on the last day; the conductor is reversing the trolley ready for the return to the city. The bus is an AEC Regent Mark III, new in 1950, on service 9 from Greenbank to Davidson's Mains. *J.H. Meredith.*

Waverley – Stockbridge – Comely Bank

All four services to Corstorphine ran via Princes Street and here No. 186 (1933-1954) is taking on passengers at the West End (Hope Street) Junction, with Binns store in the background. The junction tracks had been disused since the closure of services 2 and 22 to Stenhouse via George Street on 13 December 1952. *23 May 1953.*

No. 310 (1923-1954) outside the station at Haymarket. Loading islands (one of which can also be seen in the previous photograph) were for the safety of passengers boarding tramcars. Haymarket was the junction for services via Dalry Road to Stenhouse and Slateford. Leading out of the picture to the right is Morrison Street which had a double-track cable tramway up to Lothian Road (see also page 21). *3 July 1954.*

Waverley – Haymarket – Corstorphine

No. 77 (1928-1954), a zoo extra, on West Coates at Murrayfield Station while on its way to Waverley Station. The board in the windscreen shows 'To and from Zoo Park'. On the right is the spire of Roseburn Free Church, built in 1868 and converted into the Bible House of the National Bible Society of Scotland in 1975. *18 April 1954.*

Waverley – Haymarket – Corstorphine

Photographed on Roseburn Terrace, No. 109 (1932-1955), a later Shrubhill car, is also a zoo extra. It has passed under the railway bridge carrying the Caledonian line to Leith from Princes Street Station. Extra trams to and from Princes Street Station were always laid on for international rugby matches. Note the overhead wires splayed outwards at the low bridge to allow the trolley to clear the tram's roof. *3 July 1954.*

Waverley – Haymarket – Corstorphine

Left: No. 22 (1935-1956, built by English Electric) is seen here on Corstorphine Road, near Riversdale Crescent, heading to the city centre *en route* to Joppa. The house on the right was a doctor's surgery. *24 May 1953.*

Below: Still in Corstorphine Road, near Western Gardens a short distance beyond Riversdale Crescent, No. 346 (1926-1955) is bound for Craigentinny Avenue. *24 May 1953.*

Waverley – Haymarket – Corstorphine

The stop at Saughtonhall Drive, the old cable car terminus, was a busy one serving a savings bank and a post office, as well as a variety of shops. No. 137 (1935-1956) was a Shrubhill-built standard car. Here, it is on a 'Premier' line, service 1 - Corstorphine to Liberton. Each depot had one or more 'premier' routes' and these normally had the best cars. At Gorgie, route 1 was premier. There were more 'best' cars than were needed for the full service and the surplus appeared on services 3 and 4 but never on 2 which served industrial areas. *24 May 1953.*

Waverley – Haymarket – Corstorphine

No. 185 (1927-1954) on service 25 to Corstorphine, photographed opposite Saughtonhall Drive Post Office and tobacconist on Corstorphine Road. In the background No. 338 (1925-1954) is reversing on the seldom used crossover. *24 May 1953*.

There was a three-track layout at the entrance to the Scottish Zoological Park on Corstorphine Road. No. 70 (1929-1955) is a zoo extra and is about to return to Waverley. A hotel complex has since been built in the zoo car park area. *24 May 1953*.

Waverley – Haymarket – Corstorphine

In this photograph, looking towards the city, there are two more zoo extras. Passengers are boarding No. 169 (1950-1956), one of the last trams to be built at Shrubhill. It will end that day's tour of duty at Leith Depot, while No. 196 (1928-1956) behind (i.e. in the foreground) will only go to Waverley. *19 April 1954.*

Waverley – Haymarket – Corstorphine

The main street through Corstorphine is St John's Road and this next stop is at the junction with Clermiston Road. No. 285 (1923-1954) is outward bound. The vintage Rolls Royce in the background is opposite Station Road. Sadly, the railway to Corstorphine from Haymarket closed on 30 December 1967. *24 May 1953.*

Waverley – Haymarket – Corstorphine

The next stop, opposite the end of Manse Road, is close by St Ninian's Church of Scotland. Passengers are boarding No. 55 (1935-1956), bound for the city centre. The shops still stand although a second storey has since been added. *24 May 1953.*

Waverley – Haymarket – Corstorphine

The Corstorphine tramway was extended out to The Maybury on 14 February 1937 and this was the last line to be built in Edinburgh. The terminus was still almost out in the country when this photograph was taken and the crew of No. 69 (1934-1956) are enjoying a rest before returning to the city and Liberton. New buildings, including the Marriott Hotel, have now changed this scene. *C.M. Wiseman, 1 October 1948.*

Waverley – Haymarket – Corstorphine

Service 2 and part-day service 22 (which was introduced in October 1946) both ran via George Street and terminated at Stenhouse. No. 282 (1923-1954) is seen here approaching the Hanover Street junction. The Clydesdale Bank is on the corner by St Andrew's Church. *J.H. Meredith, 31 May 1952.*

George Street or Princes Street – Haymarket – Stenhouse or Slateford

The next junction is at Frederick Street where No. 337 (1925-1953) is seen here on service 2 with the statue of William Pitt in the background. Until 31 May 1952 the statue looked down on service 24 tramcars which came in from the right, turned left into George Street, continued to St Andrew Square and returned via Princes Street and Frederick Street passing the statue on the far side. Today the centre of George Street, where the tram tracks were, is used for car parking. *8 August 1952.*

George Street or Princes Street – Haymarket – Stenhouse or Slateford

Trams on service 4 came up from Piershill via London Road and York Place into St Andrew Street. No. 64 (1924-1953) is seen here from the corner of Princes Street, passing the office of the Bulletin, a weekly newspaper, and the Grand Restaurant. *28 December 1952.*

George Street or Princes Street – Haymarket – Stenhouse or Slateford

After the West End junctions it was a straight run from Shandwick Place to Haymarket. No. 80 (1933-1955) is seen here passing Coates Crescent on its way to Princes Street. The tram has just left the temporary stop made necessary by road works nearby. *8 August 1952.*

George Street or Princes Street – Haymarket – Stenhouse or Slateford

At Haymarket Station the services to Stenhouse and Slateford turned left into Dalry Road. No. 362 (1929-1955) is probably a football extra to Ardmillan Terrace, serving the Heart of Midlothian F.C.'s Tynecastle ground. The side boards are for tram service 4 and the driver is talking to the regulator, who would have been on duty from early morning to late evening. Cable trams once linked Haymarket with Lothian Road via Morrison Street to the right by Boots. The tracks were used to get cars to and from Tollcross Depot. When the cables were superceded, the tracks in Morrison Street remained *in situ* for many years. The Haymarket Bar is now in the building behind the tram. *8 August 1952.*

George Street or Princes Street – Haymarket – Stenhouse or Slateford

The Stenhouse and Slateford routes divided at Ardmillan Terrace, seen here with the walls of Dalry Cemetery to the right and the railway bridge in the distance. This carried the Caledonian line to Stirling, Leith and Barnton and closed on 30 April 1962. No. 319 (1924-1953) is on service 3 to Stenhouse. *8 August 1952.*

George Street or Princes Street – Haymarket – Stenhouse or Slateford

Continuing towards Stenhouse along Gorgie Road, trams would reach Gorgie Depot. No. 165 (1935-1956) is at the junction with Westfield Road and the entrance to the depot, just ahead of the tram, was a double track to the left between the nearest buildings. *8 August 1952.*

George Street or Princes Street – Haymarket – Stenhouse or Slateford

No. 337 (1925-1953) taking on passengers for the city in Stenhouse Road, at the corner of Stenhouse Drive. The building behind the tram is the Snow White Laundry, which has since been demolished and replaced by the Business Banking House. The terminus of the cable line was nearby in Gorgie Road at Chesser Avenue – a short distance ahead of the tram – but the link from there to Slateford, although authorised, was never built. *8 August 1952.*

Left: The Stenhouse route was extended by just under half a mile to Saughton Road, later renamed Saughton Mains Street, on 20 July 1930 and No. 339 (1925-1953) is seen here at the terminus. Note the 'Via George Street' board in the front window. A further extension to the city boundary was never built. The newly built Saughton Mains housing scheme is in the background. *8 August 1952.*

Below: On the Slateford Road No. 332 (1925-1954), on the summer extension to King's Road, passes over the bridge at Shandon Place. The chimney of the Caledonian Brewery is behind the tram. The railway is the ex-Caledonian line, now electrified to Carstairs. The Slateford tramway from Ardmillan Terrace, originally a single line with loops and electrically worked from 18 June 1910, was never cable-powered. *8 August 1952.*

George Street or Princes Street – Haymarket – Stenhouse or Slateford

At Hutchison Place, not far from the terminus, two passengers have just alighted from No. 80 (1933-1955). The destination screen has already been changed to King's Road, the summer terminus. The spire of St Cuthbert's R.C. Church is in the background. *8 August 1952.*

George Street or Princes Street – Haymarket – Stenhouse or Slateford

This view at the foot of the Mound was taken a year after that in *Volume 2 – The South* (p. 30), but is closer to Princes Street. No. 204 (1935-1956) is on service 27 from Firrhill while the other tram on service 23 is swinging out of Princes Street ready for the climb up the Mound and on to Morningside. *11 April 1955.*

Against the background of the tall buildings of North Bank Street, No. 183 (1927-1955) is on its way down the Mound to Hanover Street. The statue in the background is the Black Watch South African War Memorial. *24 May 1953.*

Princes Street or Mound – Tollcross, Firrhill and Colinton

After passing over George IV Bridge, the trams turned right into Lauriston Place, where No. 237 (1936-1956) is seen by the entrance to the Royal Infirmary, since closed. In the background is the University Medical School, where both my aunt and father studied. *19 April 1954.*

Princes Street or Mound – Tollcross, Firrhill and Colinton

No. 83 (1935-1956), on service 27 to Firrhill, a short way further on from the location of the previous photograph. *19 April 1954.*

Princes Street or Mound – Tollcross, Firrhill and Colinton

Returning to the city, this photograph shows a section of the other route to Tollcross and the Colinton area – used by services 9 and 10 - via Leith Street and Princes Street. No. 54 (1940-1956) is on service 10 on Leith Street, approaching the junction shown in the next photograph. *10 April 1955.*

Princes Street or Mound – Tollcross, Firrhill and Colinton

No. 175 (1934-1955), on service 9, has turned out of Leith Street into Princes Street on its journey to Colinton. This was a major intersection of routes with services going to the right off the picture, via the Bridges to Newington and Liberton. The silver-painted kiosk housed a pointsman who controlled all the points here from a small electric console. Unfortunately there are no trams to be seen in Waterloo Place as the Portobello and Musselburgh routes had been discontinued on 13 November 1954. *10 April 1955.*

Princes Street or Mound – Tollcross, Firrhill and Colinton

The Scott Monument towers over a busy scene in Princes Street. Passengers on the loading island are waiting to board No. 40 (1937-1956), on service 9 for Colinton, while No. 184 (1928-1955) is heading for Stanley Road. Following behind is No. 274 (1923-1954) on service 9 from Colinton. *3 July 1954.*

Princes Street or Mound – Tollcross, Firrhill and Colinton

The West End on an almost deserted Easter Sunday morning, with No. 211 (1941-1956) turning into Lothian Road *en route* to Colinton. The slip board in front of the driver shows 'via Leith Walk' for service 10. *18 April 1954.*

Princes Street or Mound – Tollcross, Firrhill and Colinton

Looking in the opposite direction from the previous photograph, No. 280 (1923-1954) on service 9 for Colinton turns into Lothian Road to pass the entrance to Princes Street Station (formerly the Caledonian station), which was later closed in 1965. The Caledonian Station Hotel is now the Caledonian Hilton. Trams on the three remaining Corstorphine services - 12, 25 and 26 - directly ahead to the right of the Rutland Bar, still had some three months to run when this photograph was taken. The policeman on points duty is possibly talking to his relief. *18 April 1954.*

Tollcross was still a busy tram junction in 1953. On this occasion No. 159 (1934-1955) from Colinton is heading into a congested Earl Grey Street. The policeman has stepped aside to allow No. 159 to proceed, thus obscuring the number of the other tram. It is No. 263 (1934-1956), one of the steel-bodied cars built by English Electric. *11 August 1953.*

Princes Street or Mound – Tollcross, Firrhill and Colinton

No. 185 (1927-1954), from Colinton on its way into the city via Lothian Road, coming off Gilmore Place junction into Home Street. *20 April 1954.*

Above: At Tollcross service 27 comes in via the Mound and here No. 236 (1936-1956), on service 27 to Firrhill, is seen in Gilmore Place. *20 April 1954.*

Right: A short distance further on in Gilmore Place, No. 83 (1935-1956) is also on service 27 as it enters the single-line section close by the Free Church and St Joseph's House. *19 April 1954.*

The single track extended as far as Lower Gilmore Place. No. 77 (1928-1954), on service 27, has the street almost to itself as it heads out to Firrhill. *11 August 1953.*

At the west end of the single line No. 33 (1927-1954) is moving onto the double track just beyond the Free Presbyterian Church of Scotland on the left. The numerous small shops on the right and the 'stop me and buy one' mirror the age. *11 August 1953.*

Looking in the opposite direction, towards the city with Upper Gilmore Place on the right, No. 48 (1950-1956) is seen on its way to Colinton. As the slip board indicates 'Via Leith Walk' it must be on service 10. *10 April 1955.*

These trams are on Granville Terrace, passing the end of Viewforth Terrace; Viewforth Parish Church is in the background. No. 148 (1934-1955) was built at Shrubhill and No. 308 (1923-1955) by Leeds Forge. Note how close to the kerb the trams ran. *11 August 1953.*

Princes Street or Mound – Tollcross, Firrhill and Colinton

The next cluster of shops is at the intersection of Polwarth Gardens and Polwarth Crescent where No. 115 (1927-1954), on service 9, is rounding the curve on its way to the city. The most interesting building is in the left foreground, a listed building dating from 1881 and a branch of the Bank of Scotland until 1998. It is now the Santangeli grocery store. *11 August 1953.*

Left: It was a straight run along Polwarth Terrace with its elegant villas until the junction with Colinton Road where No. 109 (1932-1955) has taken the curve on its journey towards the city centre. Behind the trees is Cranley School. *24 May 1953.*

Below: At Craiglockhart Station the Union Canal ran alongside the tramway, behind the wall on the left of the photograph. Today, the railway - ex-North British and still used for freight - still runs under the road and the canal, just ahead of the position of No. 98 (1923-1954) here. Craiglockhart Station, beyond the shops to the right of the tram, closed on 10 September 1962. *24 May 1953.*

The Craiglockhart cable tramway terminated at 'Happy Valley', close by Craiglockhart Ponds. No. 34 (1933-1955), on service 27 for Granton Road Station, is standing on the crossover. *24 May 1953*.

Princes Street or Mound – Tollcross, Firrhill and Colinton

Left: Electric traction was introduced as far as Craiglockhart Station on 15 April 1923 and extended soon afterwards to the old cable terminus. It was further extended to Colinton on 21 March 1926. No. 326 (1924-1955) was one of twenty English Electric trams and is seen here in Colinton Road at the intersection with Craiglockhart Avenue. *24 May 1953.*

Right: Another view at the same location with No. 330 (1924-1954) on service 27. Craiglockhart Hill and a golf course are nearby to the right. *24 May 1953.*

Above: At Firrhill services 9 and 10 continued round the corner and then down towards the valley of the Water of Leith. Here, No. 196 (1928-1956) is approaching the corner, heading towards the city. *24 May 1953.*

Left: Firrhill is reached by a steady one-mile climb from Craiglockhart Station. Service 27 terminated here and in this view the conductor has already turned the trolley of No. 171 (1923-1955) ready for the return journey. *24 May 1953.*

Above: No. 75 (1927-1955) on the last three quarters of a mile to the terminus, a pleasant run on a road bordered by trees and a wide grass verge. *24 May 1953*.

Left: The driver of No. 182 (1928-1954), on service 10, has just pulled away from the stop on his way to the city. Redford Barracks, to the right, and Merchiston Castle School, to the left, were served by the stops on this part of the route. *24 May 1953*.

Princes Street or Mound – Tollcross, Firrhill and Colinton